Bessie Lawrence

Thanksgiving and Other Poems

Bessie Lawrence

Thanksgiving and Other Poems

ISBN/EAN: 9783744711074

Printed in Europe, USA, Canada, Australia, Japan

Cover: Foto ©Thomas Meinert / pixelio.de

More available books at **www.hansebooks.com**

THANKSGIVING

AND

OTHER POEMS

BY

AGATHA.

NEW YORK

G. P. PUTNAM'S SONS

182 FIFTH AVENUE

1880

CONTENTS.

THANKSGIVING,

OTHER POEMS.

———

THANKSGIVING.

In a valley far from the noisy town,
The old farm-house stands low and brown.

Year by year has the summer sun
And the winter storm its work well done,

Till from door-stone broad to roof-tree high
It seems a relic of days gone by.

Patches of moss on the shingles grow,
Last year's nests in the porch below;

I

Swallows build in the chimney wide ;
Lilac bushes grow just outside ;

Their clusters of purplish blossoms fair,
Filling with perfume the soft spring air.

Bearded grain, and tasseled corn,
Wave in the breath of each summer morn ;

While the ripened apples softly fall
In autumn days by the orchard wall.

Children's voices are heard no more
Happy at play by the kitchen door.

One by one they have grown, and gone,
And the old folks now are left alone,

With figures bent, and whitened hair,
And wrinkled faces that once were fair :

Eyes needing spectacles to see,
And steps not spry as they used to be.

Bound by the ties that hold the heart
Of the old brown house they seem a part.

*   *   *   *   *   *   *

Knitting in hand in her rocking-chair,
"Mother" muses on days that were.

Every click of the shining steel,
As she sets the seam, or binds the heel,

Takes up the stitches thick and fast,
In the golden web of the days long past.

She sees in the orchard a tiny mound,
Level now with the earth around :

Her one wee daughter, sweet and fair,
She laid to rest under daisies there ;

Fifty years ! but it seems a day—
Living, she too had been old and gray.

Her memory lives, as in those young days,
"The baby" with pretty, winsome ways.

A tear-drop gathers and dims her sight,
And falls unseen on the needles bright.

*   *   *   *   *   *   *

" Father " dozes o'er paper or book,
Smoking his pipe in the chimney nook ;

With a frequent glance at the swaying chair,
To be sure that mother is resting there.

Reading the news by his own fireside,
He scarcely dreams that the world's so wide.

He has sent his sons to do their part
In the money-getting busy mart :

Four stalwart men, and he thinks with pride
There were no such boys in the country side.

He lives in them again to-day,
Since his youth and strength have passed away.

*   *   *   *   *   *   *

Oh, the golden heart-warming autumn days !
The air is full of a dreamy haze :

So quiet the noisy brooklets seem,
We hear their dashing as in a dream.

The sloping hill-sides, and mountains grand,
In a blaze of glory gorgeous stand,

Red, and yellow, and golden brown,
A mass of color fluttering down :

Hues that an artist ne'er can trace—
Nature's own for October days.

Load by load the fragrant hay
Has been gathered in and stowed away ;

Wheat, rye, oats, a goodly store,
Bundled and thrashed on the broad barn floor ;

Big golden pumpkins piled up high
For the winter's feed, and the luscious pie ;

Bins in the cellar, filled with care,
Spitzenberg, greening, and russet rare ;

New sweet cider sipped through a straw—
Nectar fit for the gods to draw.

*   *   *   *   *   *   *

There's a dream of snow in the frosty air ;
The skies are gray, and the fields are bare ;

The whistling wind, as it creeps around,
Has a sort of sorrowful sighing sound.

Boughs of green, that have filled up high
The fireplace in summer days gone by,

Are cast aside ; and morn and night,
The hearth-fire blazes warm and bright.

There's bustle and stir at the old home farm :
Some potent spell works its magic charm.

From cellar to garret a sense of cheer
Pervades the home-like atmosphere.

The very smoke curls in joyous rings,
And leaps to its airy wanderings.

Savory odors float from afar,
When the oven door is left ajar ;

And the cupboard shelves are loaded down
With flaky pies of a golden brown.

The fire burns bright in the "keeping-room."
Chambers above are all aboom

With "feathered star," and "rising sun,"
"Job's trouble," "diamond," and "herring-bone."

Works of art, tho' they be less fair
Than picture fine, or sculpture rare.

In the front porch oft does "mother" stand,
Shading her eyes with her withered hand ;

Anxiously watching the lowering sky,
Where sullen clouds scud swiftly by ;

Shutting the door, and saying low,
" I'm afraid we're bound to have some snow."

" Father " comes in from out of doors—
He's "done the milkin'," and "seen to the chores ; "

He rubs his hands at the blaze so bright—
" I'm afeard it'll be a teejus night ;

" But the cattle are housed, and the comin' storm
Will find all tidy, and snug, and warm.

" I sort o' hope we won't have snow ;
It don't hardly seem as it could be so—

" That to-morrow Thanksgivin' Day will come,
And all the children are comin' home."

Yes ! back once more to the old fireside—
Isaiah the eldest—his father's pride,

A middle-aged man with grayish hair,
And a face that shows some lines of care.

A banker—rich—they always stand
A little in awe of his wife so grand :

She isn't used to their country way,
And simple manners of every day.

Stephen too, with his gentle bride—
His parish is in the country side.

'Twas a happy day when his mother heard
His preaching of the Holy Word

From the old church pulpit perched so high—
His boyish wonder in days gone by.

Tho' the others are loved, and ne'er forgot,
In her heart he has always the warmest spot.

Captain William, their sailor boy—
How he used to shout his " Ship ahoy ! "

In his dreams, and wake them all from sleep—
His home is now on the restless deep ;

But his ship is in ; he'll anchor lay,
To keep with them Thanksgiving Day.

And noisy Robert, full of glee,
As a college boy will ever be :

The youngsters think it a lucky day
When "Uncle Bob" will lead their play.

They're sure to have the best of fun,—
Mother hopes they're coming, every one.

Such bunches of dill and caraway,
Such huge seed cookies find their way

To little hands from her pockets deep,
Are secrets grandma alone can keep.

On the earth's broad bosom, bare and brown,
The snow falls softly, lightly down ;

Tossed by the wind, in many a whirl
The feathery flakelets creep and curl ;

Drape the boughs of the forest pine
In many a graceful pendulous line,

And seem in their purity to cling
Like a benison to everything.

But if all without is bleak and drear,
Within is comfort and happy cheer.

The huge fire logs in the chimney wide
Crackle and blaze as in gleeful pride.

Spread for the feast the table stands,
The work of cunning and skillful hands.

Ye lovers of ceramics draw near ;
A tempting treasure waits you here.

Faience, Wedgwood, and Dresden fine,
Lowestoft, Canton, may all combine.

No such gems 'mong them all I see,
As in "mother's" best set of mulberry.

Only on state occasions rare
Is ever displayed this service fair :

It was "father's" gift on her wedding-day—
Not a piece broken or given away.

She looks with pride on the purplish bands,
Wipes a speck of dust with her wrinkled hands,

And hopes that "Isaiah's wife will see
Her table's as nice as need to be."

* * * * * * *

Who shall picture the tempting array
Of dainties that graced the board that day ?

Who can forget the frolic and fun
That followed when the meal was done ?

Games for the youngsters of maddest glee,
Uncle Bob leading the revelry ;

While the old folks talked in the fire-light's glow
Of other Thanksgivings they used to know.

All at home ! not a single one
From the happy circle lost or gone.

When another year shall bring this day,
Father and mother, passed away,

Their life-work done, keep hand in hand
Their harvest home in a better land.

But the children visit the well-known spot—
The old brown house is not quite forgot.

And children's children hear them tell
Of the old home days they loved so well.

Over all the land in East and West,
All that is purest, noblest, best,

Throbs in the hearts that warmly glow
With thoughts of Thanksgivings long ago :

And memory's magnet links the chain
That draws each wanderer home again.

A DREAM OF SUMMER.

Oh, the yellow, yellow buttercups !
  How the meadows are studded over—
Flecks of gold 'mid the crimson and white,
  Satin leaves 'mid the blossoming clover :
Softly blue is the summer sky,
  All the air is heavy with sweetness,
And the restless heart beats satisfied
  Hushed with a sense of life's completeness.

Listen how merrily wavelets sing !
  Over the white stones how the brook dashes !
Graceful willows bend over the bank,
  Kiss the water in softest plashes ;
Cool little nooks where the shadows play,
  Under the dancing leaves reclining ;
A slumberous murmur in all the air—
  The saddest heart must cease repining.

In the hazy distance the mountains blue—
    Bluer cloudlets their tops caressing,
Tenderly folding their rugged peaks,
    Like a life folded in love's blessing.
Threads of silver adown the green
    Mark where the cascades fall and glisten,
Thundering down through the mountain gorge,
    When only the quiet moon may listen.

Pink and white petals that fall in showers
    Wealth of velvety apple blooming,
Dashing the green with soft flecks of white,
    Filling the air with rich perfuming :
Grasshopper's chirping, and cricket's song,
    Lazily welcome each new-comer ;
Heaven above us, and beauty around,
    Speaking peace in a dream of summer.

THE TRAILING ARBUTUS.

My darling, beautiful blossoms !
  I know just where they grow—
In a little spot on the hill-side
  Where the sun-rays melt the snow.

The glossy leaves half hide them,
  And the snows around them cling ;
They stand at the door of winter
  To welcome in the spring.

So modest in their growing,
  So fragrant and so fair,
As I pluck the tiny blossoms,
  They perfume all the air.

To my sad heart tired with waiting
  They speak like the voice of song,
Like the trembling prayer that rises
  The cool church aisles among.

But most of all I love them,
  And my heart with longing fills,
When I think how in other spring-times
  They grew on my native hills.

I know each spot in the forest,
  Each sunny glade and nook,
Where in spring-time nature opened
  And showed us her wondrous book,

With its green and lovely border
  Of ground and prince's pine,
And each page traced with the graceful
  And delicate spiral vine.

Set in the midst like a picture,
  My tiny blossoming gems,
More precious than the rarest
  In monarch's diadems.

Tho' my fingers cannot gather
  My gems 'neath an April sky,
My heart can always hold them ;
  They can never fade or die.

2

CLOUD PICTURES.

Not traced by human fingers,
   Nor hung in the halls of art,
Are the paintings, rare and olden,
   Which satisfy the heart.

But when the golden sunset
   Gleams with its mellow rays,
Kind angels draw the curtains
   Which hide them from our gaze.

Shadowy forms of loved ones
   Stand where the cloud rifts part ;
Eyes that we used to worship
   Speak to the aching heart.

Oh, lips of crimson sweetness !
   Oh, cheeks like the lily fair !
Oh, form of matchless beauty !
   Oh, masses of waving hair !

My heart grows wild with longing
As I lost in wonder gaze,
While memory brings before me
The joys of other days.

The darkness falleth, falleth,
From the pinions of the night,
Hiding the sweet cloud pictures
From my eager, thirsty sight;

But in my soul their beauty
Shall never more decay,
And from my life their sweetness
Shall never pass away.

THE LACE-MAKER.

In and out, and around about,
  Over the bobbins the white threads flew ;
Loop by loop the delicate mesh,
  Leaf by leaf the tracery grew.

Dark and dreary the dismal room :
  Scarcely a glimpse of the sunny sky,
Hardly a sound from the street below
  Reached her ears where she sat so high.

Her hair in the sun was golden brown,
  In the shade a glossy chestnut red,
And it lay a mass of wavy light
  Coiled round the small and classic head.

Tiny hands and form petite,
  Coarse stuff gown such as peasants wear—
A queen could not with a sweeter grace
  Have sat in the straight and high-backed chair.

Still as she wove the pattern grew—
  Feathery ferns and bracken leaves,
Water-lilies with trailing stems,
  Nodding grasses, and wheaten sheaves.

Still she wove, while her brown eyes filled
  With tears, as her free thoughts sped away
To mossy banks in shady woods,
  Where her childish feet were wont to stray ;

To ponds where the water-lilies grew,
  By the gray old mill where she used to roam ;
And fields of nodding and waving grain,
  Where the reapers chanted their harvest home.

Still she wove, and the rare design
  Was a wreath of roses wet with dew,
And the skillful fingers deftly wrought,
  While thread by thread the petals grew.

But the tears fell fast, and she sobbed aloud,
  For as she wrought, the roses fair
Were such as a loving hand had placed
  In days of old on her shining hair.

His trembling fingers scarce could hold
　The fragrant spray with its pearly dew.
Was it the echo of words he said?
　"Darling, I'll be tender and true."

Did the grave yawn wide its black abyss?
　Was it the cold world came between?
Or, from the dim and shadowy past,
　Is it the fragment of a dream?

Poor tired heart, that has borne so well
　Its burden of grief, and fear, and wrong!
Eyes that have wept such bitter tears!
　Tiny hands that have toiled so long!

The task is done—the roses fair
　And feathery leaves she downward casts,
Blend in a mass confused and wild—
　In sleep she forgets the sorrowful past.

In her dreams she murmurs soft and low
　The story that's old, yet ever new;
A step comes bounding up the stair—
　"Darling, I'll be tender and true."

The brown eyes open in sweet surprise,
  Scarce she credits the marvelous tale ;
But the roses fair and the lilies white
  Lie soft and pure on her bridal veil.

MY PICTURE.

In a sunny smiling valley
Where the river, singing ever,
In a joyous measure hastens on its pathway to the
sea,
There's a picture, rare and olden,
That in all its beauty golden
Comes in hours of doubt and sorrow like a benison
to me.

By the swiftly-flowing river,
Where the sunbeams leap and quiver,
Stands an aged oak outspreading all its branches far
and wide ;
And about its roots unseemly
Softest mosses growing greenly,
Spreading in their emerald beauty, close down to the
water's side.

.   Daisies yellow, nodding clover,
Dot the meadow grasses over,
Lilies blooming in the sunshine flecked with spots of
crimson red ;
And, uprising from the meadow,
Bright in sunlight, dark in shadow,
Orchards waving cool and shady, and the blue sky
overhead.

Oh, the mountains, grand and hoary !
Never ancient song or story,
With its most romantic legends, so my deepest being
thrills,
As the strong and rugged beauty,
Like th' unswerving path of duty,
Grand, and glorious, and solemn, of my own loved
native hills.

On the mossy bank reclining,
Through the branches intertwining,
I can catch the shining glimmer of the ripples as they
play ;

And can watch the green trees waving,
And the fleecy cloudlets laving
In their light the mountain summits where the dark-
ling shadows stray.

Oh ! had I an artist's finger,
With what happiness I'd linger,
Over every light and shade that of my picture forms a
part ;
But I carry it unbroken,
Nature's own eternal token
Of her sympathy and kindness, deeply painted on my
heart.

ORIGIN OF THE LILIES OF THE VALLEY.

Back from the gleaming Dover sands,
Where the sunbeam scorches the shingly strands ;
Back from the softly-lapping reach
Of the tide, as it crawls to the shelving beach ;
Back from the sullen, angry roar
Of the white-capped waves that beat the shore ;
Shut in by the hills that tower so high
On every side 'twixt earth and sky,
A valley nestles, hid like a bird
In its leafy nest, or a loving word
Deep in a heart by sorrow broken,
Cherished with tears, as a precious token,
That tho' the world may its grief forget,
Kindness in some soul lingers yet.

The grassy meadow is starred with flowers
That open and close to mark the hours ;

In the sun rays bright the painted gems
Sparkle like myriad diadems ;
Waving branches above the brook
Bending, as in a mirror look,
Nodding quietly to the fair
And graceful image reflected there.
Surely was never so sweet a spot,
Far from the world, by the world forgot.

But if the valley by day seem bright,
How wondrous is it by pale moonlight !
A thousand times rarer its beauties seem
Glistening under that silvery sheen.
The waters tinkle like silver bells—
Low whispers sigh from the distant dells—
There are spells and charms on every hand ;
'Tis a spot for elves—a fairy land.

Long years ago, on a moonlit night,
When the valley shone with a radiance bright
As the rays that shot from the silver veil
Of the wondrous prophet of Eastern tale ;

While the wind harp's music was low and sweet,
The moments passing on noiseless feet,
Each marked by the opening of some rare flower,
The cereus bloomed—'twas the midnight hour.
Straightway the air seemed full of sound
From every nook in the hills around,
From every grotto and bosky dell,
From secret niche in blossoming bell ;
With step so light, not a single blade
Bent to show where a foot had strayed ;
Nor a drop of dew that had sparkled bright
Was brushed by gossamer garments light ;
With melody not of earth, like the strains
That echo in sleep over dreamland's plains ;
Bathed in a strange and shimmering light,
The fairy folk came to their festal night.

Tiny sprites like a thistle bloom—
Drapery light as a waving plume—
Elfin forms like the feathery down
Of the dandelion's seedling crown :

Full many a stately minuet
They must walk ere the moon shall set :
Full many a waltz of maddest glee,
Full many a galop de revelrie.
Fairy fingers close entwined,
They float like a breath of summer wind :
And hark ! on the air rings a chorus gay—
'Tis the drinking song of the elves at play.

Elf and sprite
    From near and far
Dancing, singing,
    'Neath moon and star ;
Fill to the brim
    Your goblets bright ;
Drink to the joy
    Of our festal night.
Ha ! Ha !
    We must away.
Dance, dance,
    Till the break of day.

Never a care
   That mortals know
Clouds our path
   As we singing go.
Fairy folk
   Are always free ;
Fill up—drink
   To our revelry.
Ha ! Ha !
   We must away.
Dance, dance,
   Till the break of day.

In the moon's soft rays their goblets gleamed,
Each cup like a line of silver seemed ;
They drained them deep, then tossed them high,
As to catch the glow from the midnight sky ;
Caught them again ere they reached the ground,
And hung them trembling on boughs around.
Then again they danced, and again they sang,
And again the silver goblets rang ;

Surely never were fairy folk in plight
More madly gay than are these to-night.

But see ! In the east one rosy gleam ;
It rests on hill and vale and stream.
A crimson glow over all is cast :
The morning breaks—the night is past.
There's a sound like a coming storm wind's moan,
Or a rush of wings—and the elves are gone.
Each leaf and flower, each drop of dew,
Sparkled with morning beauty new.
Nothing remained of the scene so gay
To tell that the elves had been at play.
Yet stay ! still trembling the goblets hung,
As from fairy fingers lightly flung ;
In their eager haste to leave the spot
The tiny goblets were quite forgot.

A little child came by that day,
Roaming wild in his restless play.
He saw the goblets trembling stand,
And touched them soft with his tiny hand.
" O pretty flowers ! what can they be ?
They're lilies of the vale," said he.

IF.

IF I could paint you a picture,
    Such as in dreams I see,
Not one of the great art teachers
    Could ever compete with me.

I'd steal the gold from the sunset,
    The azure from heaven's own blue,
And the roseate tints from the dawning,
    When the morn peeps blushing through ;

And looking out from the canvas,
    A pair of blue-gray eyes
Should answer your questioning glances
    With an eager, sweet surprise.

A low, broad, childish forehead,
    The hair brushed smoothly down—
A hint of gold in the sunlight,
    In the shade a chestnut brown.

A shy mouth, arching and drooping,
　So sensitive to a word ;
That laughs in careless gladness,
　Or trembles when tears are stirred.

I have painted a word picture—
　The portrait of a face
Fair with all outward seeming,
　Pure with all inward grace.

And yet this little child face,
　Simple as it may seem,
Is rare with a soulful beauty,
　That comes but in a dream.

MARGUERITE.

" He loves me." Pretty floweret,
  With petals soft and white,
Say, were you sleeping when he came
  Across the fields last night?

We were walking in the gloaming ;
  He left me at the bars ;
Did you hear the words he whispered
  Under the quiet stars?

"He loves me not." Oh daisy,
  You would not cruel be ;
There was no other maiden
  To bear him company.

You grew beside the footpath ;
  He brushed you passing by ;
You must have heard what name he breathed
  In that unconscious sigh.

"He loves me." Snowy blossom,
I knew you'd not deceive :
A voice so pure and charming
Speaks what one must believe.

But men are so deceitful,
One must not trust, they say ;
But you'd trust, daisy, would you not,
His words of yesterday ?

"He loves me not." Sweet daisy,
Did you look up in his eyes,
And were their glances false or true,
Under the quiet skies ?

Ah me ! Was ever maiden
In such uncertain plight ?
How shall I,—Hush ! he's coming !
What will he say to-night ?

THE CHAPEL IN THE FOREST.

ALL wreathed in leafy greenness
    The chapel door stands wide,
Its strong supporting columns
    The oaks that grow beside.

No foot-fall sounds within it
    On marble porch or aisle ;
Up from its floor of mosses
    Sweet blue-eyed violets smile.

Its stainèd windows shimmer
    Rare as the gift of kings,
When through the leafy branches
    Fair night the moonlight brings.

The winds, its mighty organ,
    Now murmuring sweet and low ;
Now sweeping all before them,
    As life's strong passions go.

The birds, its sweet choir voices,
   They chant a matin song ;
Or warble vesper chorals
   When evening shades grow long.

No white-robed priest stands waiting
   With book and bell to intone :
Low in the forest chapel
   I kneel to God alone.

My lips no words can utter,
   But my eyes are full of tears,
And my heart aches with its burden,
   Of doubts, and hopes, and fears.

So, trusting and believing,
   What peace shall crown my day,
When in God's forest chapel,
   I kneel to weep and pray.

LONGING.

Oh stately ship ! slow sailing from the bay,
  Move slowly on thy path—one moment wait,
And take a message from my longing soul,
  Ere yet you pass beyond the Golden Gate.

So smooth the ripples play around your prow,
  So clearly blue the smiling sky above,
So soft the winds that gently fan my brow,
  Thou'lt bear it safely to the land I love.

'Tis this : I miss the grandeur of its hills,
  Its sunny vales, and brooklets mad with glee,
Its long bright days full of all calm delights,
  And nights replete with beauty's harmony.

I miss its mighty rivers' rush and flow,
  Its foaming torrents, sparkling waterfalls ;
And, rising in their solemn majesty,
  Imperious and grand, its granite walls.

I miss the flowers that grew in every nook,
  Tho' others may be thought by far more fair ;
The yellow jewels nodding by the brook
  To me are dearer than these blossoms rare.

Oh white-winged ship ! God speed thee on thy
    way !
  Grant thee fair breezes, calm the treacherous
    main ;
So longingly my anxious heart will wait,
  My sad eyes watch thy coming once again.

Bring me a breath from off my native hills,
  Fill thy sails full of my free mountain air,
Catch the rare tints of Eastern sunset skies,
  Paint on thy canvas scenes so bright and fair.

Come to me laden with the breath of flowers
  That used to fill my tiny baby hands ;
Bring me a branch from the old maple tree
  Beneath whose shade the little cottage stands,

Kind angels guard thee on thy trackless way,
　And keep me safe, who for thy coming wait,
Till I shall see thy swift sail once again
　Pass, homeward bound, within the Golden Gate.

MY SECRET.

In the deep red heart of a queenly rose
  I breathed my secret with many a sigh;
The velvet petals with dewdrops shone,
  But they only nodded royally.

Then I whispered low to a zephyr light,
  " I love my love, but she loves not me ; "
But the balmy breeze with odors sweet
  Swept softly onward to reach the sea.

I cried to a bird on a waving bough,
  "Know you my love?"   In a trilling tone
He chirped and chittered, "I seek my mate,"
  And left me once more sadly alone.

Then I caught the strain of a glorious song,
  And I gave my secret to music's sway ;
But the strain grew sad, and the measure wild,
  And died in the twilight dim away.

It rose on the wings of my evening prayer,
   As I lowly knelt in the sunset's glow.
Did the angels whisper the answer back ?
   "Oh, fearful heart, go tell her so."

Then I kissed it down on her ripe red lips,
   I looked in the depths of her smiling eyes,
And I clasped her close with a strong true arm,
   While my glad heart laughed in its sweet surprise.

Oh, rose and bird !   Oh, breeze and song !
   I care no more that ye scornful be ;
My soul is full of all calm content,
   I love my love, and my love loves me.

ASLEEP.

Hush ! winds that oft so coldly, rudely blow,
  Breathe soft as zephyrs o'er a summer lake ;
Come from the south with sighing sweet and low ;
  My heart's asleep—I tremble lest it wake.

Ye birds that carol loud your joyous song,
  Twitter it low to-day among the leaves ;
And whet not once your brightly gleaming scythes,
  Ye sturdy reapers of the golden sheaves.

Oh, laughing brooklet ! linger not I pray ;
  My heart stirs strangely in its restless sleep ;
But hasten on thy mad tumultuous way—
  If thou should'st waken it, it would but weep.

I could not bear that it should moan and sigh,
  And beat with longings all unsatisfied ;
I could not bear that it should tell me oft,
  " Life is so dark, I would that I had died."

So I have lulled it with a song to rest—
  Have satisfied it with a promise sweet,
That when it waken, if it will but sleep,
  It shall find life more noble and complete.

Come, gentle flow'rets, perfume all the air—
  Fragrant hepatica, and gentian blue,
Anemone, and snowy lily rare,
  And sweet wild roses sparkling o'er with dew ;

That so its slumber may be long and deep—
  If thou a fairy-land of sleep canst make,
Filled with all beauty both of sound and sight,
  And brightest dreams, it will not care to wake.

It could but prove my promise all untrue ;
  It must not waken till, beyond the skies,
We meet the purer and the truer life
  In store, when the eternal morn shall rise.

Then only can we look for faith and trust,
  Friendship sincere, and love that's true and strong.
Here we can only weep, and hope, and pray,
  When sorrow makes the days seem dark and long.

So wait I till these weary days are o'er,
  And the fair night, in all its glorious dress,
Precedes the dawning of that brighter morn,
  When my tired heart may wake to happiness.

A PERFECT DAY.

THE fleecy clouds lie soft against the blue,
As if the angels o'er the sapphire walls
Lean silent, while beneath their folded wings
   There comes a glint of glory gleaming through.

The balmy air, laden with odors sweet,
Blows cool and freshening from the distant hills,
While the soft murmur of the rustling leaves
   Drops lightly, like the sound of dancing feet.

The mountain brook comes dashing down the glen,
While graceful ferns and golden jewels bright
Mark where amid the silence on it flows,
   Far from the crowded haunts of busy men.

From out the orchards spread on either side
The rosy fruit peeps through the glossy leaves,
And the blue smoke curls gracefully aloft,
   Where the old farm-house door stands open wide.

The sheaves are stacked on either side the way,
The grain, well ripened, waiting to be stored,
While all the meadows, flecked with blossoms bright,
 Are fragrant with the scent of new-mown hay.

God's benison, descending from above,
Rests on the earth, and peace fills all the air ;
And o'er my heart the gentle influence steals,
 The chrism of a pure and perfect love.

A love that knows no change—that feels no fear—
That looks beyond earth's clouded, dreary night
To heavenly days, when God's eternal smile
 Shall make each perfect morning bright and clear.

A PICTURE.

SHE stood below me where the vines
  Shadowed the face so wondrous fair ;
The glancing sunbeam left a ray
  Of glory on her golden hair.

Her sweet brown eyes looked up to mine
  With all a child's simplicity ;
Yet in their depths I fain had read
  More than a passing thought of me.

The tiny hands and soft white arms
  Closely the trellis work entwine :
The rosy lips hold richer feast
  Than amber clusters from the vine.

I stooped and whispered, soft and low,
  So sacred seemed the words to me,
"Kiss me !" I shook with sudden fear,
  And then I waited, trustfully.

4

Quick, like the glow of early morn,
 The blushes spread o'er cheek and brow ;
She bends that fair and graceful head—
 Those brownest eyes are dewy now.

And then she raised to mine the lips
 That should be mine forever more ;
And all the earth, and air, and sky,
 Was glorious as ne'er before.

Through all my life, in good or ill,
 Till hushed in silence of the grave,
My lips with glad delight will feel
 That first warm kiss my darling gave.

ON THE DEATH OF A PET BIRD.

THE song is hushed, and the singer
　　Silent forevermore ;
The stillness steals upon you,
　　As you near the well-known door.

The gilded cage in the window
　　Swings high in the morning air ;
But the tiny home is empty—
　　There is no birdling there.

No yellow-throated birdling,
　　Whose life was a gush of song,
That pealed like joy-bells ringing
　　The busy days along.

Scarce sadder would our hearts be,
　　Scarce heavier with care,
Were there an empty cradle,
　　Or a tiny vacant chair.

What wonder if the hot tears
   Rise fast and overflow,
When we think the song was ended
   By a sudden cruel blow.

Is there no heaven for birdlings?
   No land of blooming flowers,
Where they may sing forever,
   Through happy golden hours?

Surely their lives and sorrows
   Are to the Father known,
Without whom not one sparrow
   Falls to the ground alone.

So fair and pure our birdlings,
   I think it well may be
The strain so rudely broken
   Shall reach eternity.

ONLY.

Only a memory! Yes, 'tis true—
  A memory of a morning fair,
When spring's sweet sunshine kissed the earth,
  And violets perfumed all the air.

Only a memory! One low word,
  Earth, air, and sky, new brightness wore ;
And lo! upon my girlish hand
  A ring I ne'er had worn before.

Only a memory! You may smile ;
  You think the tale is old, I ween ;
But 'twas the spring of life and love,
  And I ? Why I was just sixteen.

Only a memory! Even now
  I feel the hot blood flush my cheek
As I recall those whispered words,
  That only dreams henceforth may speak.

Only a memory !   Yet I sigh
  When others laugh to greet the spring ;
And you have wondered why I weep
  To hear the earliest robin sing.

Only a memory !   Life is full
  Of earnest deeds, not vain regrets ;
Yet even now my soul grows faint
  At breath of woodland violets.

Some time, if I be strong and true,
  Will eager tones say low to me,
" This is the glad fruition, love ;
  We have no need of memory."

MEMORIES.

Thank God for pleasant memories ;
  Through the dim mist of tears
The saddened eyes behold again
  The joys of vanished years.

The flowers we cherished tenderly
  With fondest care are dead ;
But o'er the paths of memory
  Their fragrance sweet is shed.

The songs we loved are ended now,
  The lips that sung them dumb ;
But oh ! how often to the soul
  Their chiming echoes come.

The friends we knew, but meet no more ;
  Ah me ! a minor tone
Marks the sad rhythm of those lives
  That battle fate alone.

How sad, without a gleam of hope,
    If we could not look back,
And live again the days that lie
    So bright in memory's track.

But hope makes glad the darkest hour,
    And by her light we see
The fairer days that are to come,
    The joys that yet shall be.

We linger fondly o'er the past,
    Each happy time and scene ;
Then looking forward, we forget
    The dreariness between.

KATE AND I.

'Twas 'neath the blossoming apple-tree,
  In the merry month of May;
A warm wind blew from the southern land,
  And scattered the leaves away.
    The snowy petals rose,
    Far in the quiet sky,
While we stood and watched their silent flight,
    Kate and I.

The fair round moon as it rose that night,
  And shone on the earth below,
Saw loving glances in hazel eyes,
  And a crimson cheek's warm glow :
    Then sweetest kisses fell—
    I'm sure no one was by—
And we were watching the fair moonlight,
    Kate and I.

Now as I sit in my cheerful room,
  All happily pass the hours :
For love weaves a garland for every day
  Of the sweetest and fairest flowers.
      I journey not alone,
        Another form is nigh :
And till death we travel cheerily on,
        Kate and I.

LEAFLETS.

Out in the forest lonely
  The leaflets are dropping down,
Fluttering slowly earthward,
  Golden, and crimson, and brown.

Fanned by the soft spring zephyrs,
  Kissed by the summer sun,
Chilled by the winds of autumn,
  Their bright brief life is done.

My darlings ! my lost treasures !
  In spring-time, oh ! how fair,
To music of the south wind
  Ye danced in balmy air.

And my tired eye grew brighter,
  My weary soul grew strong,
While like the harp's low music
  Murmured your gentle song.

Now must we part forever?
Oh, mountains, grand and tall,
Your gorgeous robes of autumn
Seem like a funeral pall.

The moaning, sighing north wind,
Sweeping through rocky glen,
Beats with my heart's sad measure
My darling's requiem.

Glorious in dying splendor,
Oh, changing leaflets dear,
My heart sighs for your beauty
In hours of winter drear.

And oft, when storm-clouds gather
I lift my heart in prayer,
That the days of my life's autumn
May be, like yours, most fair.

LOVE'S TEACHING.

Teach me a new name, darling,
  One that is tender and true,
Full of the heart's own music,
  And worthy even of you.

It must be bright as the sunshine,
  Clear as the summer sky,
And fragrant as rarest perfume
  The balmy breeze wafts by.

It must be like your own true nature,
  Noble, and grand, and free ;
With a power like the storm-king's voices,
  And a murmur of the sea.

It must have a sound of music,
  The breath of a tearful prayer,
As I call my heart to worship
  Its idol enthroned there.

It must be soft and gentle,
　　Like the falling of the snow ;
But ever warm and ruddy,
　　Like the crimson fire-light's glow.

So if, in all your learning,
　　One such a name you know,
Teach me to know it, darling,
　　That I may call you so.

But if in earthly naming
　　There be none so deep and high,
I'll ask the listening angels
　　To whisper it from the sky.

O FAITHFUL HEART!

WHAT tho' the winter snow lies deep,
And all the fairest blossoms sleep?
The spring will come with sun and rain,
And all the earth will smile again.
    O faithful heart !
    Love on, trust on.

What tho' the clouds so darkly frown,
And pitiless the rain comes down ?
They soon will part, and heaven's own blue
Soft and serene will shine on you.
    O faithful heart !
    Love on, trust on.

What tho' in dreams you live again
Long weary hours of grief and pain ?

Lo, see ! the morning breaks, and joy
Will soon each hateful dream destroy.
    O faithful heart !
    Love on, trust on.

What tho' you long for tender tone,
And loving glances all your own ?
That longing rises through the air,
And answer comes to each sweet prayer.
    O faithful heart !
    Love on, trust on.

For, far beyond the glowing skies,
The holy land of promise lies ;
And each true heart will find the bliss,
The rapture that's denied in this.
    O faithful heart !
    Love on, trust on.

ETCHINGS.

Apple-blossoms sweet and fair,
Once I wore them in my hair :
Mem'ry bells ring silently,
When I think who placed them there.

Lilies of the valley, say,
Can I e'er forget the day
When he whispered, soft and low,
"Darling, you are pure as they"?

Star forget-me-nots so blue,
Would I had been ever true !
"You have stolen," once he said,
"For your eyes their heavenly hue."

Cherries ripe and rosy red,
"They are like your lips," he said ;
But the ripened cherries fell,
And the summer days are dead.

5

Over all the winter snows
　Silently and softly fell,
Clothing in a mantle white
　Every bud and lily bell.

So the summer of my heart
　Yields to winter's frost and snow ;
But upon the canvas oft
　Memory's pictures come and go ;

And I fancy we shall find,
　When we reach some happier sphere,
Angel hands have hung them there,
　Where the light is pure and clear.

LEONA.

CHILD of the darksome forest,
    Where art thou fled ?
The wreath I wove for thy glorious brow
    Is faded—dead.
The moon comes out from the fleecy cloud,
  And shines on the silver sea ;
Leona, my pride, my spirit bride,
    Come back to me.

Maiden with jetty tresses,
    And soft brown eyes,
Hast thou left me here to pine alone,
    And sought the skies ?
The violet blooms in the shady dell,
  And the daisy sleeps on the lea ;
Leona, my pride, my spirit bride,
    Come back to me.

My lonely heart is crying
      In vain for thee :
Only the wind's low sighing
      Answereth me.
The clouds are parting—thy form I view—
   Come hither, mine own, to me :
Leona, my pride, my spirit bride,
      I come to thee.

A RETROSPECT.

OH eyes that weep such bitter tears !
Once, long ago, in happier years,
  I deemed thy brightness ne'er could fade ;
I fondly thought each coming day
Would find thee ever bright and gay,
  Nor sorrow e'er thy glances shade.

Oh fingers, soft, and white, and fair !
I little thought that grief and care
  Would cause thee so to intertwine ;
Or cling so closely to my breast,
To still within this wild unrest,
  This longing, aching soul of mine.

Oh heart that loved so fond and true !
I dreamed, as many others do,
  Thy joyous life was wisely given ;

Those careless hours of sunny youth,
When first I pledged thy fondest truth,
   Seemed like a foretaste here of Heaven.

Too soon came sorrow, care, and pain,
My heart will ne'er be young again,
   Nor feel the joy it used to know ;
Only beyond the far-off skies
I'll meet, with smiles of sweet surprise,
   Such bliss as once was mine below.

MY KING.

My monarch wears no jeweled crown,
  No rubies red, nor diamonds rare ;
Only upon his royal brow
  Some curling waves of chestnut hair.

No ermined robes of rank and state
  My monarch's manly form adorn ;
Only the quiet ease and grace
  Of noblemen by nature born.

Within the hand that presses mine
  Is held no badge of high behest,
His only sceptre is his smile,
  Type of the law I love the best.

He sits upon no dazzling height,
  No courtiers around him bend ;
His throne is in my faithful heart—
  My loving thoughts his titled friend.

No stern decree of monarch's power
 To traitor subject e'er is given,
Only the glance of soul-lit eyes,
 Within whose depths I find my heaven.

Oh, noble monarch !   Better far
 To know one heart will loyal be,
Than reign unloved, mistrusted, feared,
 'Mid hollow pomp and revelry.

Oh, happy heart that owns thy sway,
 What joyous praise my lips shall sing !
While every blissful moment shows
 How grandly noble is my king.

MY QUEEN.

I worship daily at a shrine,
 'Tis not in old cathedrals grand,
Nor where tall minster towers arise,
 Or humbler sacred fanes may stand.

No crucifix is there upreared ;
 No beads with Aves set between ;
My altar is my hearthstone bright—
 I pay my homage to its queen.

Fairer is she than sylph or fay,
 Tender as love itself to me,
When, at each close of busy day,
 She softly sits upon my knee.

Her hair as chestnut's coat is brown,
 Waving in shades of burnished gold ;
And oh ! the light that, soft and fair,
 Lies hidden in each shining fold.

Her brow is pure as evening's sky,
   And calm as lakelet's gentle breast,
When on its bosom tranquilly
   The water-lilies sink to rest.

Her eyes—oh, sweetest, tenderest eyes !
   My soul into their depths can fall,
Can sink and lose itself, and then
   Still find itself best loved of all.

To those dear orbs of azure hue
   Love's holiest missions here are given :
Within their changeful, melting blue
   I catch my first rare glimpse of Heaven.

The sea-shell's rarest, faintest pink
   Plays o'er her cheek so smoothly round ;
Her lips are ripe with kisses sweet ;
   Her voice is music's thrilling sound.

Her strong true heart beats all for me ;
   The same when joy's bright numbers roll,
Or sorrow's waves flow drearily,
   Or dash in madness o'er the soul.

Oh, kingdom blest ! Oh, beauteous queen !
  Could I thy praises fitly sing,
My words should bud on time's cold shore,
  But blossom in eternal spring.

A RAINY NIGHT.

DARK is the night and drear !
  The heavy drops of rain
Fall fast and faster still
  Upon my window pane.

No moon, no stars, to-night—
  I drop my curtain down ;
The very lamp's dim light
  Seems almost like a frown.

Alone ! how fast they come,
  Thoughts of the days gone by,
Trooping through memory's halls,
  A silent company.

Oh, loves of long ago,
  Stand back ! I cannot bear
To see ye, pale and still,
  Standing before me there.

A RAINY NIGHT.

What tho' *'twas* childish love?
  Has love of riper years
Been half so strong and true,
  So free from doubts and fears?

O lips that I have kissed!
  'Tis well ye too are come
To mock me with your smile:
  Before you I am dumb.

Strong hands that I have clasped,
  I feel your pressure now:
Rest ye forgivingly
  Upon my saddened brow.

Reproach me not, ye eyes
  Whose depths I never knew:
Your light was once my heaven—
  Would I had been as true.

Hark! how the rain comes down!
  The wind is moaning wild,
A requiem for the days
  Strong, true and undefiled.

Tears?   Well, I'll let them fall—
　Perhaps they'll leave more bright
The eyes whose depths are stirred
　This rainy, dreary night.

MY HEAVEN.

WHERE is my heaven ? Not in the realms of ether,
  Where fleecy clouds lie soft against the blue,
And where at even-tide the golden glory
  From angel wings comes softly shining through.

Not in the joyous ring of baby laughter,
  Or flowing ringlets to the breezes cast :
Not in the memories, sorrowful and tender,
  That fill the soul from out the shadowy past.

Not in the sheen of rarest gems that glitter
  On beauty's brow, or tremble on the sight
In caverns deep, like the pale stars that twinkle
  Serene and still upon the brow of night.

Not in the far-off land of the hereafter,
  Where loved ones wait us who have gone before ;
Nor where the echoes of the grand Te Deum
  Sound down the arches from th' eternal shore.

Not in all richest gifts of earthly naming,
  Nor any thought of bliss beyond the skies ;
Not in glad hopes their full fruition claiming.
  My only heaven is in my darling's eyes.

DREAMING.

Oh, the days of long ago,
When my heart beat to the glow
Of hopes that greet us only in our youth's bright day ;
When every morn was bright,
And the stars shone every night,
And every month was joyous as the laughing May.

Oh, the jewels by the brook,
In the quiet, shady nook,
How I loved the pleasant corner where my ear-drops
grew.
Never pearls that bound my hair
Seemed to me one half so fair
As the graceful golden blossoms that my childhood
knew.

Oh, the elm-tree branches wide,
Drooping o'er the sparkling tide,
6

Casting shadows on its surface when the sun was
    high :
        Oft I lay beneath their shade,
        Watching how the shadows played,
While the fleecy clouds were sailing 'cross the azure
    sky.

        Oh, the tender words of love
        Whispered in the silent grove,
When the moon was beaming brightly on the earth
    below :
        How they echo in the heart,
        Till the burning tear-drops start,
While memory brings the accents I no more may
    know.

        Clouds are oft around my path,
        But one joy my bosom hath,
And many times has sadness fled before the glow
        Of the peace that fills my heart,
        When I sit and muse apart,
On the happy, happy days of the long ago.

TO BELLA.

WOULD you know what you are like?
When the wine begins to flow,
When the bubbles sparkling break,
And we cry, "Vive la Cliquot!"

Just the first warm rosy glow—
'Tis the life of the champagne:
Gone, like youth's first, freshest bloom,
It can never come again.

In the soft, still summer morn,
Ere the sun begins to shine,
There's a tint in all the east,
Tender, roseate, divine;

Just a hint of brighter hue—
Light that ushers in the day:
On the cool, fresh morning air,
Quick it vanishes away.

Deep within the rose's heart,
  Hidden close by petals fair,
There's a secret spot, secure,
  Sacred to its perfume rare.

Nature's breath, so fragrant, pure,
  Mystery unknown to art ;
Only nature's lovers know
  Secrets of a rose's heart.

There's a single throbbing tone,
  Full of passion, full of pain,
Tremulous with loving joy,
  Ever sounds a low refrain.

Through the mystic melody,
  In each chord so full and strong,
Speaking to the inmost heart—
  'Tis the voice of glorious song.

Living glow, and roseate blush,
  Perfume rare, and music's soul,
Can but feebly shadow forth
  All your wondrous sweet control.

These, in all their richness rare,
  All their perfectness you are ;
But to me, who love you well,
  Something dearer, sweeter far.

THE KING-FISHER.

Translated from the French of André Theuriet.

THE king-fisher shoots like an arrow of blue :
   His flight spring perfumes follow
To his nest, which gleams in the cool fresh morn,
   Half hid in a leafy hollow.

In the limpid lake he dips his wing,
   Still wet with dew-drops sparkling,
Where from early morn he has sought his prey,
   In reedy hollows darkling.

His plumage is charged with the fragrant breath
   Of the newly-mown sweet clover :
While it catches the hue of the morning's sky,
   With a soft gray clouded over.

As he nears his nest in the old tree root,
   His free flight untiring keeping,
His piercing cry makes the echoes start,
   And wakens the birdlings sleeping.

Naught they have learned of that great wide world
  ˮSurrounding their leafy dwelling ;
But their tiny breasts, half nude as yet,
  With a sudden hope are swelling.

They venture forth upon trembling wing,
  Where reeds and rushes quiver ;
And where like flashes of spotted light
  The fish dart down the river.

Some instinct within them strangely stirs,
  Prompting the bonds to sever :
A plunge—a cry—and they are lost
  To the reedy nest forever.

GRANTED.

"What do you mean by love?" she asked.
  "I know it must be something grand;
If you'll explain a little bit,
  I'll try so hard to understand."

O ruby lips! O satin cheek!
  Blue eyes of wonder open wide;
So near your gaze who could explain?
  "Well, why don't you begin?" she cried.

"True love," I answered, "is a rose
  That blooms when other flowers are dead;
And scatters fragrance far and wide."
  "But roses have big thorns," she said.

"True love is like an inward fire,
  That burns and burns by night and day."
"What! ne'er goes out at all?" cried she.
  "'Twould scorch one's very breath away."

"True love is an impetuous stream
  That on and on forever flows ; "
"Oh, dear ! " she pouted, "that's too cold ;
  I shiver to my very toes."

"True love is like a chain, that binds
  So close, for life and death as well : "
"Love like a clanking chain? " cried she.
  "'Tis only fit for prison cell."

I closely clasped her hand in mine,
  Her wee, white, timid, fluttering hand :
"Now listen—look into my eyes,
  And try to rightly understand.

"True love is like an earnest prayer,
  That heartfelt rises to the skies ;
That's hardly breathed by trembling lips,
  And overflows in tearful eyes."

She shyly raised her eyes to mine,
  Then swiftly bowed her golden head :
Her sweet lips trembled with their joy—
  "Why, one should grant a prayer," she said.

TO MADAME MARIE ROSE.

Oh, the roses ! The roses !
  A world of rare perfume,
A world of blending color,
  A world of beauteous bloom.
We scarce can tell the fairest,
  So many fair we see ;
But there is one—the rarest,
  We call it Rose Marie.

Gentle, and sweet, and loving,
  As the Wild Rose wet with dew
That blossoms in green country lanes,
  The rose our childhood knew ;
Or the Cinnamon Rose that budded
  Beside the garden gate,
On which we leaned in the twilight,
  A coming step t' await.

Fair as the waxen petals,
  The spotless buds half blown,
That ever in the raven hair
  Of matchless beauty shone :
With a tender, varying color
  That to the cheek will start,
Like the delicate shades that linger
  In the Tea Rose's deepest heart.

A grand and glorious meaning
  In the dark eyes' slumbrous fold,
Deep, full, intense, a hidden fire,
  Like the heart of the Cloth of Gold :
The charming, graceful presence
  Disguise can ne'er conceal :
A perfect blooming, like the flower
  Of the peerless Marshal Neil.

But this queen of my rose garden,
  This blossom of my choice,
Unlike all other roses,
  Speaks in a wondrous voice ;

A tone that touches and echoes
  My heart-strings all along,
Till they stop beating, to listen—
  'Tis the voice of glorious song.

Sometimes a love-song tender,
  To be sung in the twilight dim—
Sometimes a prayer just whispered,
  Or a grand cathedral hymn ;
Sometimes a gay French chanson,
  Or a sparkling barcarole,
Sometimes a strain of grand despair,
  To shake the very soul.

It matters not—the music
  Is ever full and free,
And the voice that charms the waiting world
  Sings tenderly to me.
Fair queen among the roses,
  Fairest of all we see,
Long may she reign, the lovely,
  The peerless Rose Marie.

ASHES.

Soft and still, cold and gray,
 A pile of ashes before me lies ;
I, motionless, wonder if they will stir
 When the first faint breath of morn shall rise.

All night long I have watched them fall,
 Softly and silently, one by one,
A gray cold mass 'neath the blackening grate,
 They have all fallen—my watch is done.

Some hours ago, when I lit the fire
 (Is it hours or years I have passed since then ?)
My heart beat high with a strong desire,
 A hope, a love, like other men.

The cheery flame leaped quick and high,
 As if it waited the touch of my hand,
And flashed a reply to my inmost thoughts,
 I almost think it did understand.

What pictures I saw in the glowing coals !
What a truthful artist bright thoughts can be !
And mine were as bright as the dancing flame,
   As they painted me pictures fair to see.

What was it that dimmed the pictures' glow ?
   A letter—a marvel of delicate art :
" We have both been quite mistaken, and so
   You must see it is better that we should part. "

'Twas a dainty sheet like a rose-leaf pale,
   Its breath of perfume filled all the air ;
Since I crushed it in my burning hand,
   There's a scent of rose leaves everywhere.

" Give it to me," the fierce flame cried.
   I smoothed it out, and I kissed it thrice,
Then laid it upon the glowing coals—
   It was burned to ashes in a trice.

O God ! how it writhed in the flame's hot grasp !
   I strove with my might its mad course to stay ;
Then I knew by the coldness I felt within,
   It was my heart that had burned away.

There is no flower when the root is dead—
 What need of hope when the heart is gone ?
So I said farewell to my hopes so bright,
 And burned them to ashes one by one.

They were sweet as the first warm breath of June,
 And fair as the blossom on Alpine snow ;
My hand was ice, and my lips were dumb,
 As I yielded them up to the crimson glow.

My fair false love, could you see them now,
 The heart and the hope that were thine before,
Would you care, I wonder, that naught remains
 But ashes, piled on the marble floor ?

The night is over—the day dawns fair—
 Below, the street echoes with busy tread ;
I open my door, and leave behind
 Only a pile of ashes—dead.

THE ROBIN RED-BREAST.

Translated from the French of André Theuriet.

I HAVE had a dream, my darling :
  Half hid in a leafy wood,
On the border of a meadow,
  A low-roofed cottage stood :
In a tall tree, white with blossoms,
  A robin, with scarlet breast,
Twitters and sings in gladness,
  As he builds his mossy nest.

The red-breast, tender and loving,
  Whose breath of joyous song,
In eager, bounding measure
  Like his life-blood flows along,
Till it bursts, a stream of music,
  From his throat, as deeply red
As the scarlet berries that glisten
  'Mong the leaves by the river bed.

His coming shall bring us gladness,
    And his nest in the beechen tree
A charm, a guerdon of fortune,
    An amulet shall be.
To our window, by tendrils shaded,
    When the day is young and fair,
His happy roulade of greeting
    Shall float on the morning air.

And when on amethyst pinions
    The night sinks slowly down,
And noiseless spreads o'er the drowsy world
    A mantle of golden brown ;
When your fair young head, my darling,
    In my arms shall cradled rest,
A softly twittered lullaby
    Will sound from the leafy nest.

When the spring time paints the hill-sides,
    And the brooklets wake and sing ;
When lilies gem the meadows,
    And there's beauty in everything ;
   7

When the sober mulberry bushes,
   Stand dressed in their robes of gray,
Still the happy red-breast carols,
   As he steals their fruit away.

When the frost with sparkling fingers
   Makes pictures on the panes ;
When the snow lies, drifted whiteness,
   Along the distant lanes ;
To a place on the hearth between us,
   To the glow of our happy home,
To our warm good cheer and affection,
   We'll bid our birdling come.

And our red-breast, ere he leave us,
   Leaves behind the frost and snow,
Will sing, as he stands in the shadow
   Of our fire-light's crimson glow :
" Through the burning heat of summer,
   Through the winter's cold and snow,
True love blooms on unfading."
   My darling, shall it be so ?

GHOSTS.

You don't believe in ghosts, you say?
  Hm. Well, I must confess, I do ;
If you had seen one face to face,
  Perhaps you might believe it too.

'Twas thus—before my glass one night
· I passed, when sudden gleaming there,
'Mong the smooth braids, I saw a light
  Upon the shade—my first gray hair.

I almost laughed aloud in scorn ;
  I would not have it so, in truth ;
Turning, I saw beside me stand
  The ghost of my departed youth.

My heart throbbed mightily—not fear
  The cause—the rather silent pain ;
The present was a dream, and quick
  The long gone days came back again.

The days when eyes were brightly blue,
　　And cheeks as red as rose in May;
Before the hot tears came that burned
　　The fair, fresh, youthful tints away.

When the young heart was fresh and warm,
　　And full of faith in God and men ;
How many bitter, bitter hours
　　Have changed the faith to doubt since then.

When each new day was new delight,
　　And every untried path a way
Through flowery fields and meadows bright ;
　　When hope grew stronger every day,

And love was warm, and always true ;
　　No fear it might grow cold or fail ;
For over all the glowing world
　　Lay youth's bright morning's mystic veil.

The phantom stood with sad, sweet eyes,
　　Seeming my every thought to know ;
While memory brought and pictured fair
　　Each glad detail of long ago.

As, fading soft within the blue,
  Melt the last tints of dying day ;
E'en as I gazed in mute surprise,
  The still, sweet presence died away.

I stretched my arms to hold it fast.
  "Come back," I cried.   "Oh ! say not so,
That youth is thus forever fled.
  Come back, I cannot let you go."

No answer but the sighing wind :
  Alone, I turned : "O spirit fair,
Some token leave "—again I caught
  A glimpse of this, my first gray hair.

No, let it lie, one silver thread
  Among the countless darker host ;
'Tis proof that I am growing old,
  And once, at least, have seen a ghost.